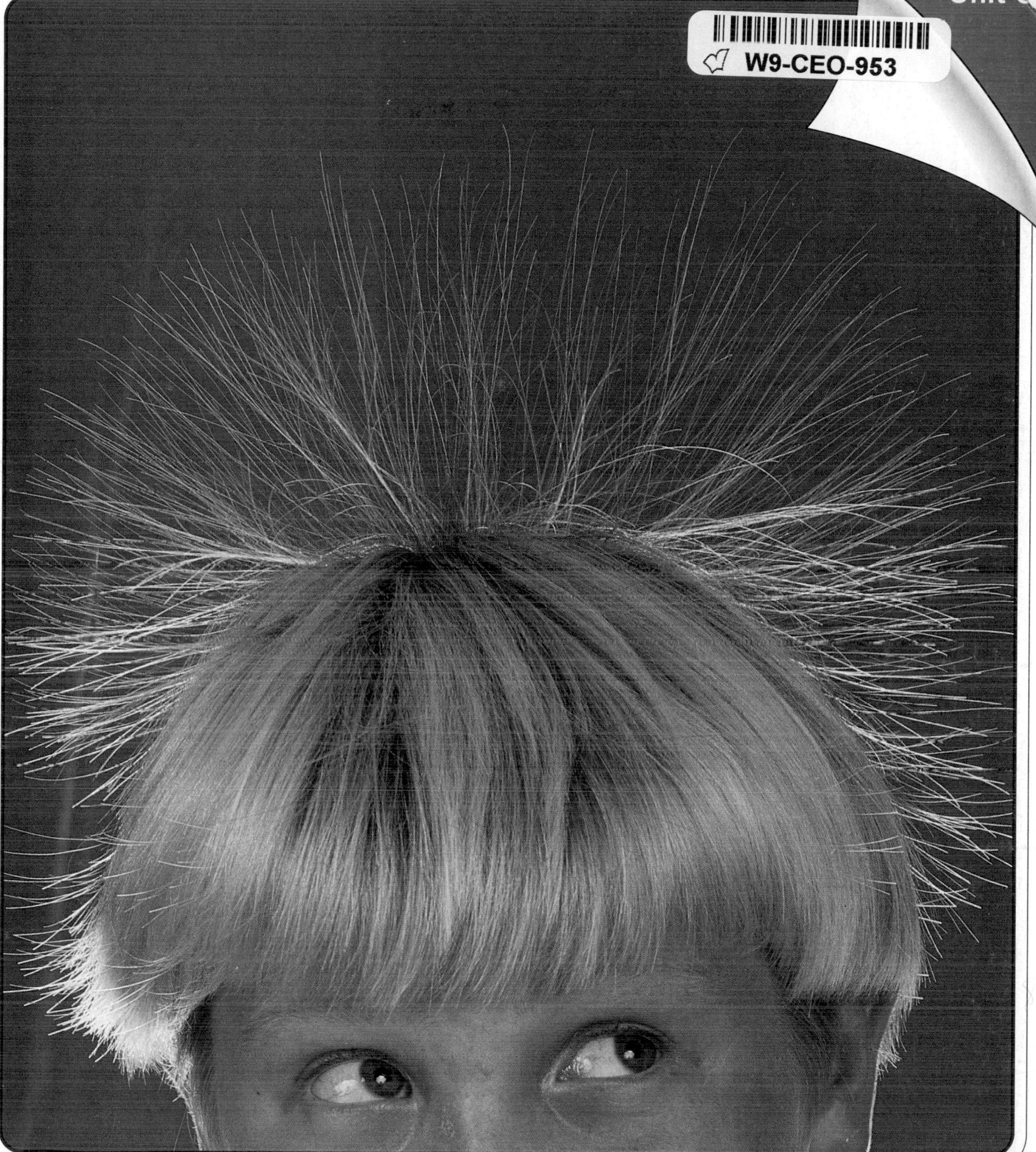

Unit C

ON AIR
abc
ABCNEWS NEW YORK

TV Studio

Welcome to a television studio. A television studio is a place where television programs are made. It is a few minutes before air time, and everyone is busy. From the visitor's gallery high up in the control room, you look down on the sound stage. People are rushing around, making some last-minute changes—adjusting lights and moving equipment.

As you look around the television studio your attention is focused on the equipment. So many different devices are needed to make a television show! They all run on electricity. Take a look at the devices shown in the picture. Can you identify any of them? Look at all the wires running across the floor of the sound stage. Can you trace the wires to the equipment?

- What is electricity?
- How is electricity used?
- How is electricity related to magnets?

ELECTRICITY

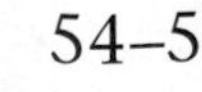

Activities

Features

Static Electricity

The television screens in the control room of a TV studio are called video monitors. The word *video* comes from the Latin word meaning "to see." You know this word if you have watched videotapes or seen a video camera.

The video monitors allow people in the control room to watch, or monitor, the pictures being taken by each television camera in the studio. Like most equipment in a TV studio, video monitors are run by electricity. Many devices in your home are run by electricity. All you have to do is plug them into a wall outlet and turn them on.

Not all electricity comes through a wall outlet. Not all electricity moves, or flows, from one place to another through a wire. **Static electricity,** for example, is an electric charge that collects, or builds up, on the surface of an object. Static electricity causes dust to collect on the screens of the video monitors in the TV studio.

In your Science Journal, write about or draw two examples of static electricity that you have seen.

ABC TV NY
Graphics Factory 143

Explore Activity

How can you tell if something has an electric charge?

Process Skills

Defining operationally, Observing

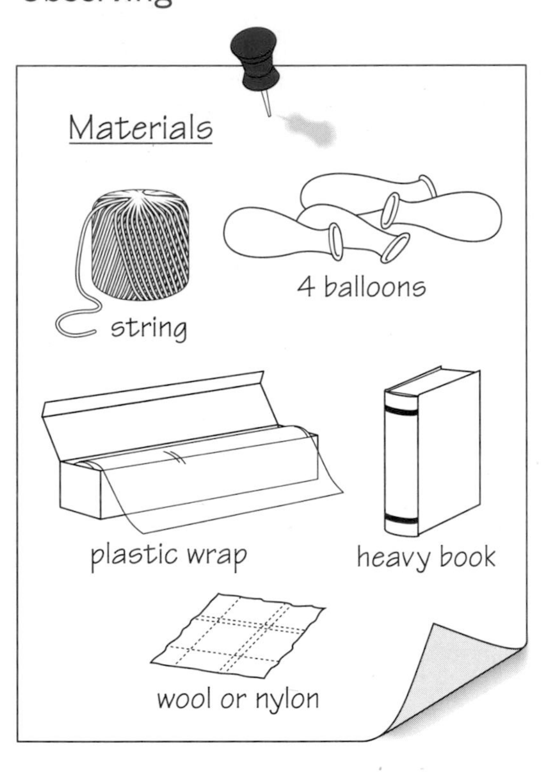

Observe and Collect Data

1. Blow up two balloons. Tie a string to each and hang as shown in the picture below.
2. Rub each balloon with the piece of nylon (or wool).
3. Bring the balloons near each other. Observe what happens.
4. Blow up two more balloons. Repeat steps 1–3, this time using plastic wrap for step 2.
5. Now bring one balloon rubbed with nylon close to one balloon rubbed with plastic wrap. Observe what happens.

Share Your Results

1. What happened when you brought two balloons rubbed with the same material close together? Did other groups get the same results?

2. What happened when you brought balloons rubbed with different materials together? Did other groups get the same results?

Draw Conclusions

What do you think happened to the balloons when you rubbed them?

Apply What You Know

Predict what would happen if you brought the plastic wrap you used and the nylon you used together. Test your prediction.

Where does static electricity come from?

Just about everything you can think of is some kind of matter. All the pieces of equipment in a TV studio are matter. Matter is made up of tiny particles. These particles contain two different kinds of electric charge—positive and negative. We refer to positive charges using a plus (+) sign. Negative charges are shown by a minus (–) sign.

Forces exist between electric charges. A force is a push or a pull. Most matter has an equal number of positive and negative charges spread evenly throughout it. The charges balance each other, so the matter seems to have no charge at all. Such matter is said to be neutral (nōō´trəl).

Be a Scientist

HANDS-ON ACTIVITY

How can you make cereal dance?

1. Place a few pieces of rice cereal in a balloon.
2. Blow the balloon up. Tie the end. Rub the balloon on your hair.
3. Hold the balloon by the knot with one hand, and touch the balloon with a finger from the other hand near the cereal. What happens?
4. ACTIVITY JOURNAL Describe your observations in your Activity Journal. Try to explain what you observed.

Have you ever removed laundry from a clothes dryer? If so, you have probably noticed how some articles, such as wool socks, stick to other articles, such as nylon shirts. This "static cling" is caused by different materials becoming charged as they rub against one another inside the dryer.

BACK HOME

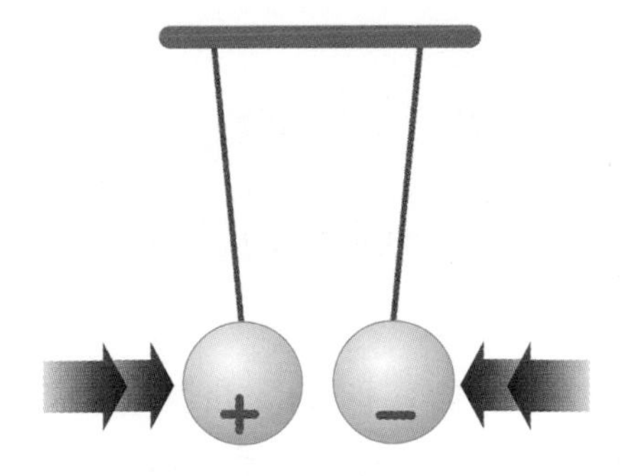

Unlike charges pull toward each other. They are said to attract each other.

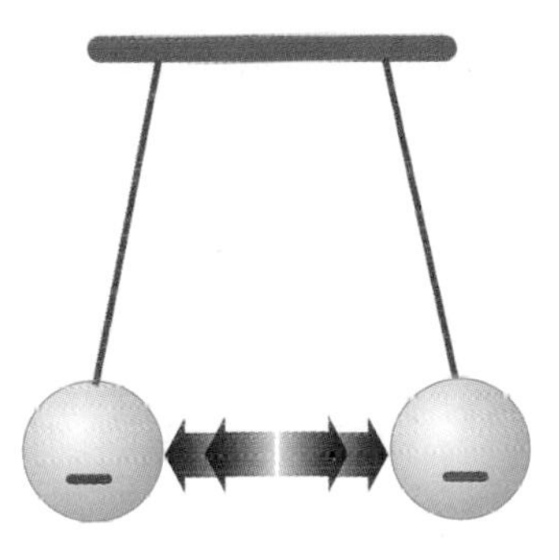

Like charges push each other apart. They are said to repel each other.

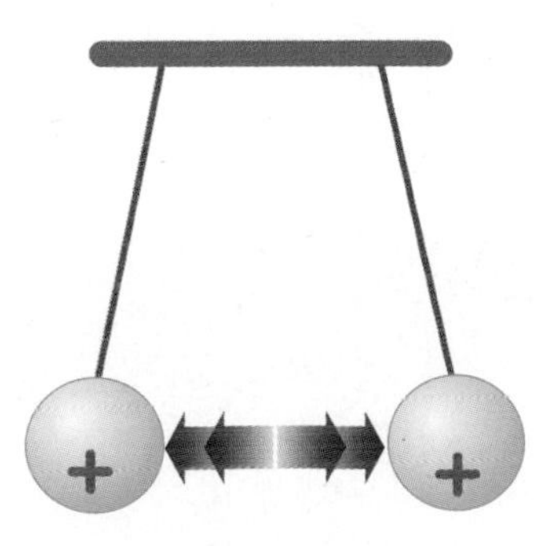

Matter becomes charged when negative charges move from one place to another. Positive charges in solids do not move. When negative charges move on or off matter, the matter becomes electrically charged.

Sometimes, negative charges are rubbed off of one object onto another. When this happens, both objects become charged. One object becomes positively charged and the other object becomes negatively charged.

How does matter become charged?

These pictures show what happens when a balloon is rubbed with wool. Before rubbing, the balloon and the wool each have an equal number of positive and negative charges. The rubbing causes negative charges to leave the wool and go to the balloon. This makes the wool have more positive than negative charges, and we say it is positively charged. The balloon has gained negative charges, and it now has more negative charges than positive ones. The balloon is negatively charged. Remember, positive charges do not move around in solids. Only negative charges move.

Sometimes a positively or negatively charged object can cause an unlike charge to build up on an electrically neutral surface such as a wall. Look at the negatively charged balloon sticking to the wall. Negative charges on the wall are repelled, or pushed away, by negative charges on the balloon. This leaves the surface of the wall with a positive charge.

Rubbing the balloon with wool gives the balloon a negative charge.

The negative charges on the balloon are attracted to the positive charges on the wall.

The attraction between the unlike charges on the balloon and the wall causes the balloon to "stick" to the wall.

You may have noticed that dust collects faster on a television screen than on other nearby surfaces. When the television is on, static charges build up on the picture tube. Dust particles in the air near the screen also become charged. The dust particles and the television screen attract each other.

Have you ever received a small electric "shock" when you reached for a doorknob or other metal object? This shock is caused by a buildup of electric charge on your body. As you walk across a wool or nylon carpet, the soles of your shoes rub against the carpet. In cool, dry weather, the result is something like rubbing a balloon with a wool cloth. Negative charges can leave the carpet, collect on your shoes, and build up on your body. When you reach for a metal object, a tiny electric spark passes between you and the object, producing a small shock.

SIDE TRIP

Science Museum

What is happening to the boy in the picture? Is he watching a horror film? Actually, the boy is taking part in a demonstration of a device found in many science museums. It is a Van de Graaff (van´di gräf) generator. It can produce a large negative charge and store it on the surface of the metal sphere.

Most science museums have many fascinating displays such as this one that help make learning about electricity fun.

What is lightning?

Lightning is one of the most familiar and dramatic effects of static electricity in nature. Lightning is also very powerful. Its charge is millions of times stronger than the charge that can shock you when you rub your feet on the floor and then touch metal.

4. Winds separate the charged particles, causing the upper part of the cloud to become positively charged. The bottom part, or base, of the cloud becomes negatively charged.

3. Swirling winds within the cloud produce tall, towering clouds, called cumulonimbus clouds.

2. Positively and negatively charged particles are spread out evenly in this cumulus cloud.

1. Warm, moist air near the ground rises rapidly. As the rising air cools, water condenses and clouds form.

5. The negative charge at the base of the cloud repels negative charges in the ground below the cloud. So, the surface of the ground beneath the cloud becomes positively charged.

6. As charges continue to build, the force of attraction between the negative charges in the cloud base and the positive charges of the ground increase.

7. When the force of attraction between the charges in the cloud base and the ground becomes too great, a powerful electric spark moves between the cloud and the ground. This is lightning.

▲ In this picture, lightning is moving between the cloud and the ground. But lightning may also move between clouds, or between one part of a cloud and another.

How are you doing?

1. Sometimes plastic wrap sticks to your hand and won't fall off. Explain how charges cause this.
2. Why does most matter seem to have no electrical charge?
3. **Think** How might matter with a negative charge be made neutral?

Television and Society

Try to imagine what your life would be like without television. Talk to some older people—perhaps your grandparents. Ask them how television has changed the way people live. It is very likely that their viewpoint will be different from yours.

The opinion of many people is that in the days before television, people spent more time talking to each other. The major forms of entertainment were playing games, reading, and listening to the radio. These activities required people to use their imaginations. They formed their own mental pictures of the people and events they read about or heard on the radio.

The opinion of people who grew up with television as part of their lives is often different. Many feel that television takes them to places and shows them things they would not see otherwise. TV brings important events from all over the world into their homes at the time those events are taking place. Overall, most people who have grown up with television feel that it has helped them to be better informed about the world around them.

Data Collection and Analysis

What materials charge easily?

Observe and Collect Data

1. Use the materials to make a device like the one shown here. Be careful when bending the paper clip. Make sure that the sides of the foil hang straight down from the paper clip.
2. ACTIVITY JOURNAL Rub the balloon with the wool cloth. Then slowly bring the balloon near the foil ball. Do not touch the ball. Observe what happens. In your Activity Journal, write the name of the item tested (*balloon*) and tell what happened.
3. Repeat step 2 with each item.

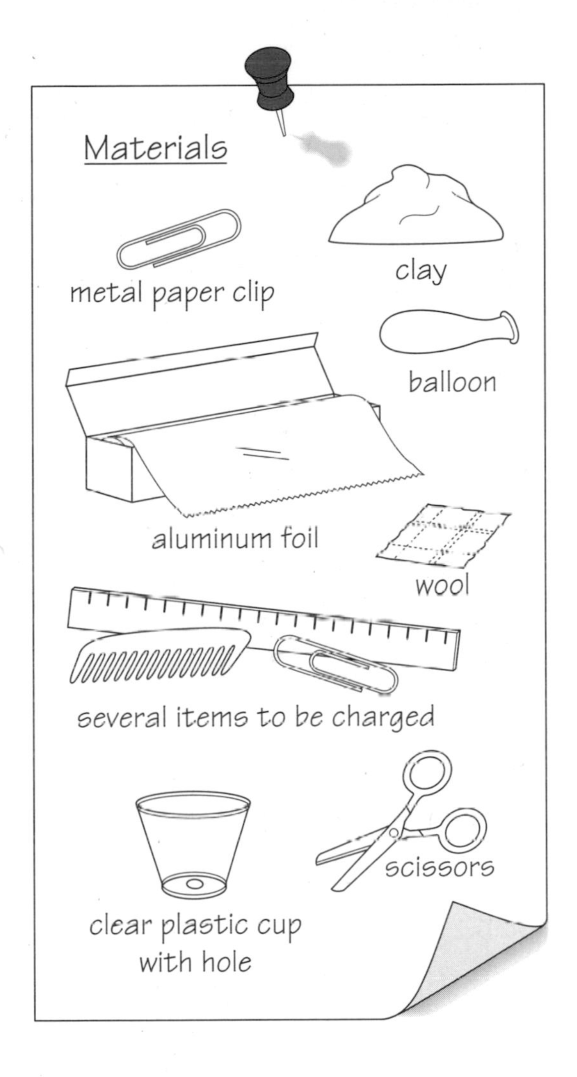

Draw Conclusions

1. What happens when you bring the charged balloon near the foil ball?
2. How can this device be used to show whether an object is charged?

Looking Back

Words and Concepts

Complete the following statements.

1. _______ electricity is the buildup of electric charges on a surface.
2. All _______ is made up of very tiny particles.
3. A plus sign (+) indicates a _______ electric charge.
4. _______ exist between electric charges.
5. Like charges _______ each other.
6. Unlike charges _______ each other.
7. Only _______ charges are able to move freely from place to place in a solid.

Applied Thinking Skills

Answer the following questions. You can use words, drawings, and diagrams in your answers.

8. After rubbing a balloon with a piece of nylon, will the balloon repel or attract the nylon? Explain your answer.
9. What must happen in order for an object to become negatively charged?
10. **Your World** Why is it more likely that a charge will build up on your body when you walk across a wool carpet than across a wood floor?

Show What You Know

How do charged objects affect uncharged objects?

Observe and Collect Data

1. Bend the coat hanger so that it will stand on a desk, as shown. Hang the plastic foam "peanuts" from the hanger.
2. ACTIVITY JOURNAL In your Activity Journal, **predict** what will happen if you bring an inflated balloon near the peanuts without touching them. Try it. Record what happens.
3. After rubbing the balloon with the wool, repeat step 2.

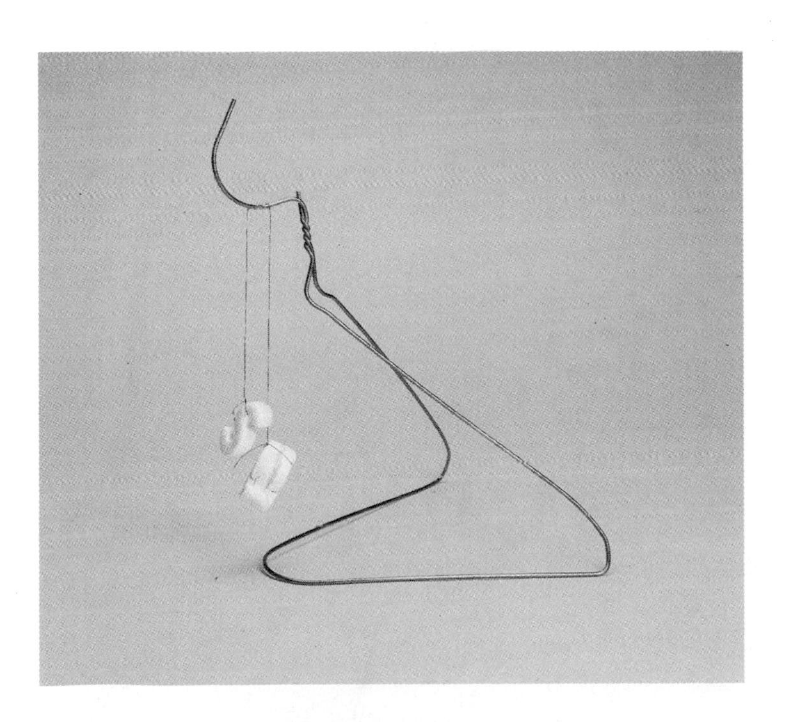

Process Skills

Observing, Predicting

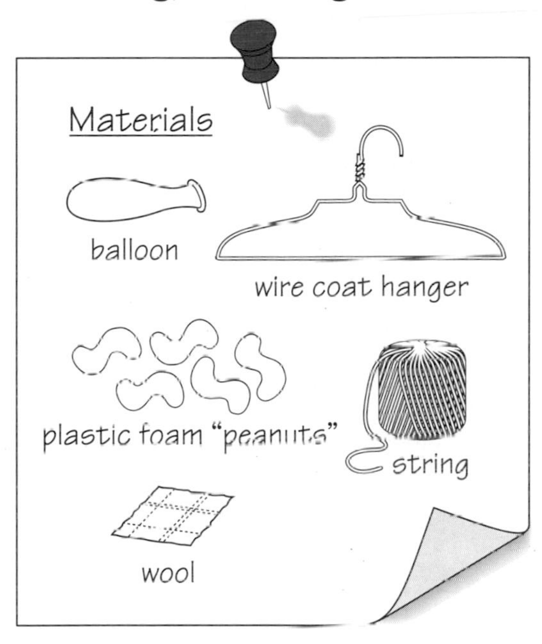

Draw Conclusions

1. How did your predictions compare with your observations?
2. Compare the action of the plastic foam peanuts in step 2 and step 3.
3. How was the balloon different in the two steps?

Chapter 2

Current Electricity

Current electricity is the kind of electricity people use every day to light their homes and run their appliances. This electricity is carried by wires like the ones shown in the picture. Some wires must be able to carry large amounts of electricity to run stoves or air conditioners. Other wires, like those in a calculator, carry very small amounts of electricity.

Many electrical devices in your home have cords, or wires, that must be plugged into a wall outlet in order to work. The same is true of many devices in a TV studio. The cameras, lights, and microphones must all be plugged in to work.

You rely on current electricity more than you think you do. How many times today will you switch on or off something electrical? If you had lived a little more than a hundred years ago, you would not have been able to find switches, plugs, or even a light bulb anywhere in the world. At that time, current electricity was not created in power stations and sent through cables to people's homes. By 1900, people were beginning to use current electricity in their homes and businesses.

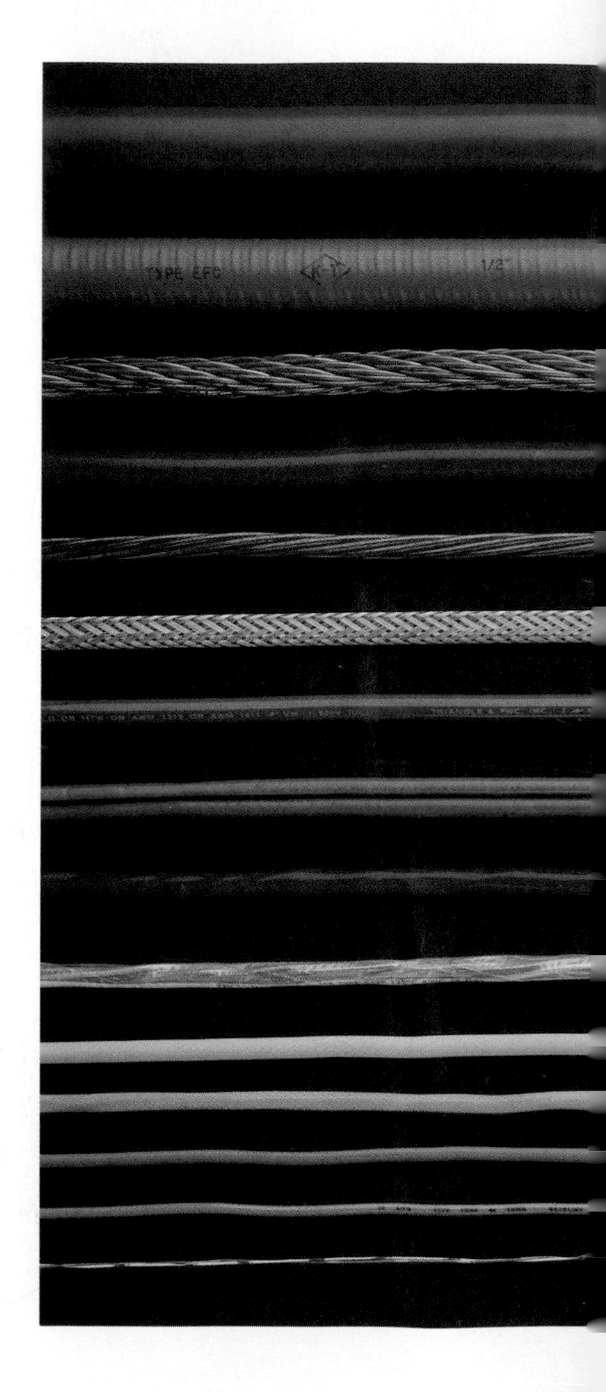

In your Science Journal, list some of the ways you use current electricity every day.

DANGER
HIGH
VOLTAGE
HCL HCL Labels, Inc. (800) 421-6710

How can you move charges?

Process Skills
Observing, Inferring

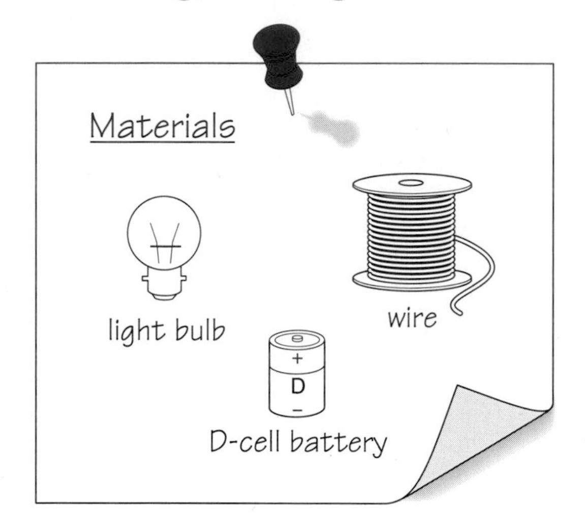

Observe and Collect Data

1. Use the wire to connect the D-cell battery and the bulb in as many different ways as you can think of.
2. ACTIVITY JOURNAL In your Activity Journal, diagram each of the ways you connect the D-cell battery and bulb. For each setup, indicate whether you think negative charges move through it.

Share Your Results

Compare your diagrams with the diagrams of other students. Especially compare the diagrams of setups in which negative charges moved. What causes the similarities or differences between the diagrams?

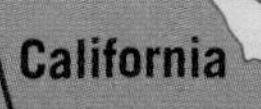

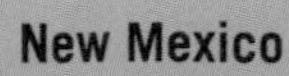

Draw Conclusions

1. How could you tell which setups allowed negative charges to move through them?
2. Why were charges not able to move through some setups?

Apply What You Know

Predict whether or not negative charges would still move through some setups if two bulbs were used.

What is electric current?

▲ When you plug something into an outlet, you tap into an electric current. The electricity flows through the plug and into the object you plugged in.

For electricity to be useful, it must be moving continuously. So static electricity is not very useful.

Recall that only negative charges can move freely from place to place in a solid. An **electric current** is the flow, or movement, of negative charges through a material. The energy provided by the moving charges is called electrical energy, or simply electricity.

Electricity can be used to do work. However, the energy of the moving charges that make up electricity must be controlled. You must be able to make electricity move and stop moving when you want. And you must be able to control where it goes.

The energy in a lightning bolt is not useful because it cannot be controlled. ▶

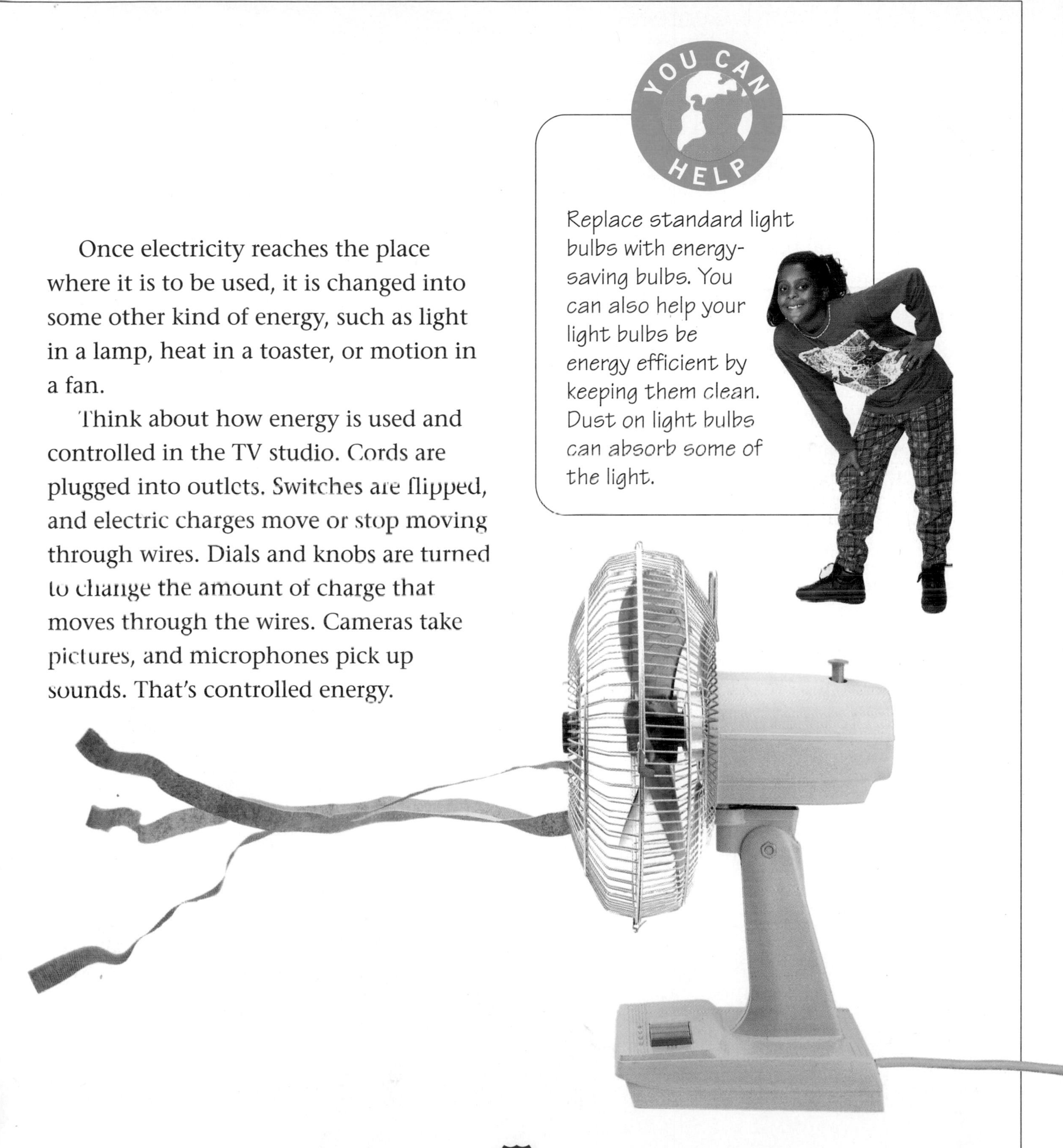

Replace standard light bulbs with energy-saving bulbs. You can also help your light bulbs be energy efficient by keeping them clean. Dust on light bulbs can absorb some of the light.

Once electricity reaches the place where it is to be used, it is changed into some other kind of energy, such as light in a lamp, heat in a toaster, or motion in a fan.

Think about how energy is used and controlled in the TV studio. Cords are plugged into outlets. Switches are flipped, and electric charges move or stop moving through wires. Dials and knobs are turned to change the amount of charge that moves through the wires. Cameras take pictures, and microphones pick up sounds. That's controlled energy.

What are conductors and insulators?

Wires are the pathways through which negative charges flow. Wires are made of materials that can carry these charges. A **conductor** is any material that allows negative charges to move through it. Metals make the best conductors. Copper is the most common metal used for that purpose. The wires used in a TV studio and in your home are probably made of copper.

Metal wire conductors are covered with insulation to prevent people from being injured by charges moving through the wires.

You may be familiar with the expression "live wire." The word *live* is used to describe any conductor in which charges are moving. Moving charges can be very dangerous. Your body is a good conductor. If you were to touch a live wire, the charges in the wire would move through your body and you would receive an electric shock. If the wire is carrying enough current, the shock can cause serious injury, or even death.

Negative charges do not flow freely through some materials. These materials are called

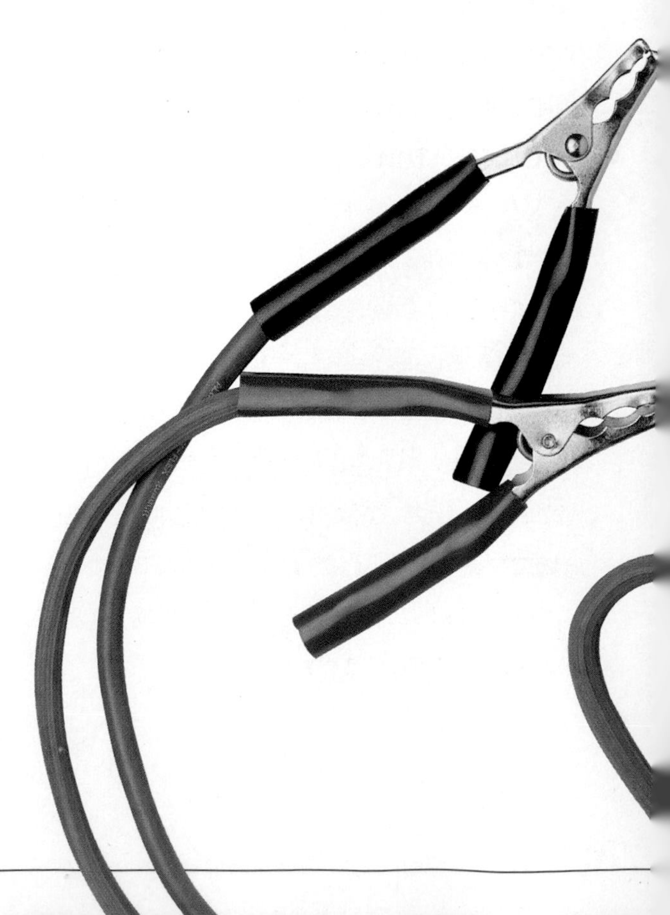

The metal cables and metal clips of the jumper cables are conductors. You are protected by rubber insulation.

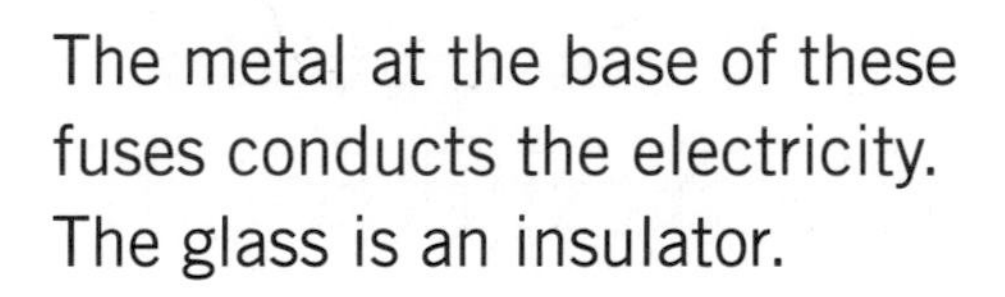

The metal at the base of these fuses conducts the electricity. The glass is an insulator.

insulators (in´sə lāt´ərz). Some good insulators are rubber, wood, glass, and certain plastics. To make electricity safe to use, conductors and appliances are covered with an insulator. This covering is called insulation. The negative charges can continue to move freely through the conductor, but the insulation will protect a person from the live wire.

As long as negative charges have a complete path to follow, they will continue to move through a conductor. But where do all these negative charges come from? Somewhere, there is a device that provides a steady supply of negative charges. It may be a huge generator at an electric power plant, or it may be the chemicals in a tiny cell that runs a wristwatch or calculator.

Be a Scientist

HANDS-ON ACTIVITY

What materials conduct electricity?

1. Make a circuit using a D-cell battery, two lengths of wire, and a bulb. Open the connection between one wire and the bulb. Connect a third wire to the bulb and the free end of the other wire. The bulb should light.
2. Open the connection between the two wires that are connected. To test a material, place it between the wires and touch the ends of the wires to the material.
3. ACTIVITY JOURNAL Test different materials. How can you tell if a material is a conductor or an insulator? In your Activity Journal, indicate which materials are conductors and which are insulators.

What is a charge separator?

Matter is usually made up of equal numbers of positive and negative charges. However, only the negative charges can move about freely in solids. When negative charges can be made to move through a conductor, such as a wire, their energy can be used to do work. The problem, then, is to separate the negative charges from the positive charges and get them moving through a conductor.

An **electric cell** is a device that separates positive and negative charges. The cell then "pushes"

Look around your house for devices that get their energy from cells. In your Science Journal, list the devices and tell what kind of cell each uses.

BACK HOME

The acid in the lemon is a chemical that can separate charges from the metal stuck in the lemon. The negative charges move through the wire conductor and make the clock work.

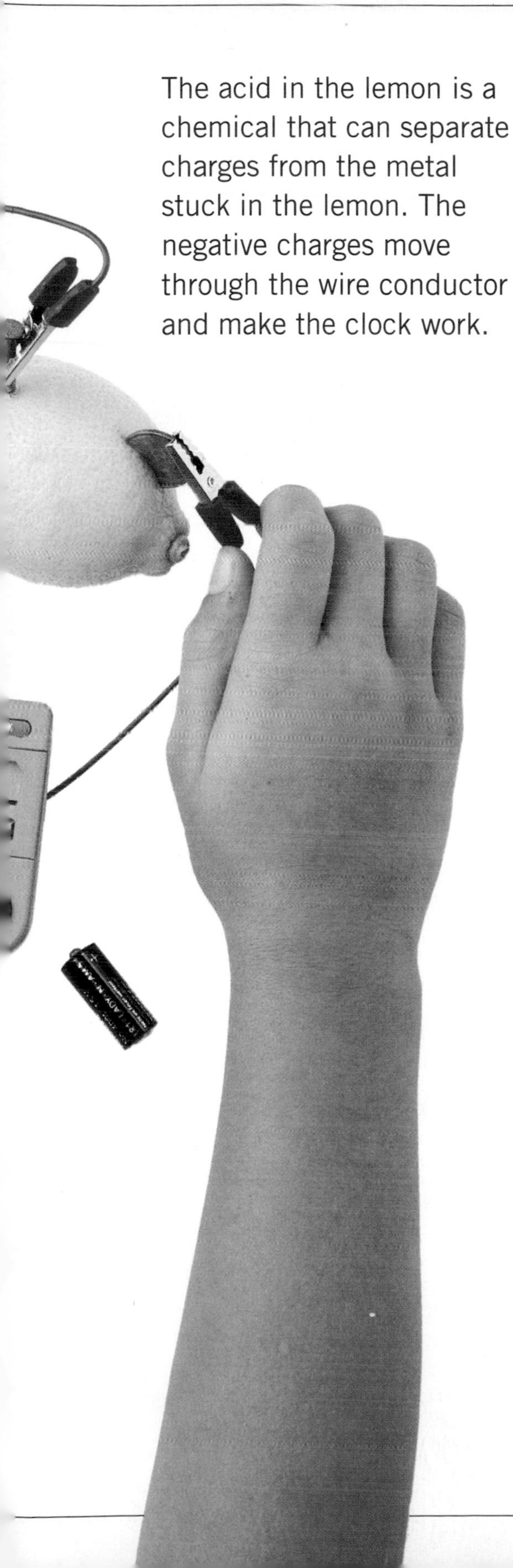

the negative charges through a conductor. The batteries you use to operate flashlights and portable radios are types of electric cells. Batteries are sometimes called dry cells.

Energy is needed to separate charges. In an electric cell, the energy comes from chemicals. In the "lemon cells" shown in the picture, the energy comes from the reactions between the acid and the metals stuck in the lemons.

In some cells, the energy to separate charges comes from light. Have you ever seen a solar-powered calculator? Light shining on the solar cells separates the charges in the material that makes up the cell. The negative charges are used to operate the calculator.

How are you doing?

1. Which is more useful—current electricity or static electricity? Explain your answer.
2. What is the difference between a conductor and an insulator?
3. **Think** Why are electric cells known as charge separators?

Lesson 2 Types of Circuits

What is a series circuit?

A path along which negative charges flow is called a **circuit** (ser´kit). A circuit begins and ends in the same place. Charges will move through a conductor only if they have a complete, or closed, path leading back to where they came from.

The picture shows a closed circuit made up of a D-cell battery, wire conductors, three bulbs, and a switch. A switch is a device used to open and close a circuit. Think about what happens when you flip a switch in your home. Electricity moves through the circuit until the chemicals in the D-cell battery are used up or until the circuit is opened, or broken. What are some ways to open the circuit?

When the switch is closed, the circuit is complete. Negative charges leave the dry cell and move through the conductors. Negative charges move through the bulbs, causing them to glow. Negative charges return to another part of the D-cell battery.

Be a Scientist

HANDS-ON ACTIVITY

How do you make a series circuit?

1. Connect two D-cell batteries and three bulbs with wires to make a series circuit.
2. When all the bulbs are lighted, unscrew one bulb. Observe the other bulbs.
3. ACTIVITY JOURNAL In your Activity Journal, draw a diagram of your circuit. Tell what happened to the other bulbs when you unscrewed one. Explain what you observed.

An electric circuit has at least three parts. One part is the source of electric energy. This can be a battery, a generator, or some sort of a power plant. A second part is the object that uses the electric energy, such as a bulb. A third part of the circuit is the wire or cable that links the power supply with the object.

The light switches in your home are the places where wires meet to connect the circuit. When flipped in one position, the switch connects the wires and completes the circuit. The light turns on. When flipped in the opposite position, the switch puts a gap between the wires so that the electricity cannot complete its path.

The type of circuit shown on the opposite page is called a series circuit. In a **series circuit,** all the parts are connected in a single path. Series circuits are simple to put together.

◀ Tiny microchips like this one are used in computers. A microchip contains an integrated circuit.

What is a parallel circuit?

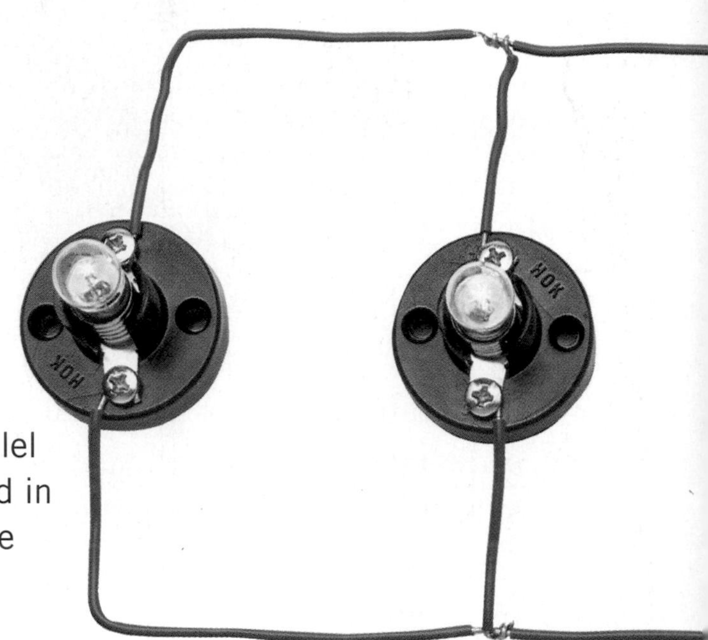

Devices in this parallel circuit are connected in a number of separate branches. ▶

Suppose you wanted to wire the electrical system in a TV studio. The simplest and quickest way to do this is to connect all the switches and outlets in a series circuit. What problems would this setup create?

Look at the circuit shown here. It has all the same parts as the circuit shown on page C30. However, there is an important difference in the way these lamps are connected. In a **parallel circuit,** the different parts of the circuit are connected in separate branches.

A parallel circuit is more difficult to put together than a series circuit, but it has an advantage. It

◀ This string of party lights is a parallel circuit. What will happen if one of the bulbs burns out?

gives charges more than one pathway to follow. Why do you think this is an advantage?

The outlets and electrical appliances in your house are connected by parallel circuits. When you plug in the toaster, you have added a part to a circuit. The toaster draws the power it needs from the electricity flowing through the circuit.

Different appliances need different amounts of power. For example, a refrigerator needs about ten times less power to run than a toaster. The difference is that the toaster is only on for a few minutes.

Be a Scientist

HANDS-ON ACTIVITY

How do you make parallel circuits?

1. Connect a D-cell battery and three bulbs with wires to make a parallel circuit.
2. When all the bulbs are lighted, unscrew one. Observe what happens to the other bulbs.
3. ACTIVITY JOURNAL Draw a diagram of your circuit. Tell what happened to the other bulbs when you unscrewed one. Explain what you observed.

How are you doing?

1. What is a circuit?
2. What is an advantage of using a series circuit? What is a disadvantage?
3. **Think** What kind of circuits, series or parallel, are used in your home? How do you know?

What is in a typical circuit?

All circuits contain conductors of some kind. Usually the conductors are wires. The type of wire used in a circuit depends on how much electric current it will carry. Usually, the greater the current, the larger the diameter of the wire and the thicker the insulation.

Circuits may also contain switches, outlets, fuses, circuit breakers, current regulators, and energy receivers. Energy receivers are the things you want to use. Some examples are a lamp, a stereo, and a TV set.

Some circuits are simple. For example, a flashlight has the four basic parts of a circuit—a source (battery), a receiver (bulb), a switch, and wires connecting these things. You may be able to see these parts when you open the flashlight. Other circuits are not simple at all. A television set, for example, may have hundreds or even thousands of circuits.

Fuses and Circuit Breakers
A circuit will become overloaded whenever too much current flows through the wire. An overloaded circuit can cause a fire. Fuses and circuit breakers are safety devices. They open, or break, a circuit that becomes overloaded. Running too many devices plugged into the same outlet can cause a circuit to overload.

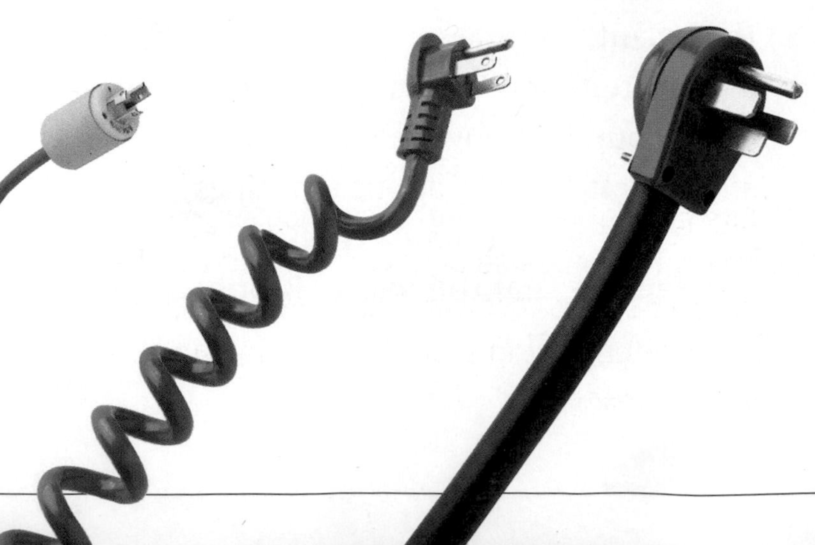

Look at the pictures of the TV studio you saw earlier. Can you see where some of the circuit parts described here are found in the studio?

Conduct a rheostat search. Study the circuits and appliances in your home. In your Science Journal, record which ones contain rheostats. Tell why the rheostat is neeed.

BACK HOME

Electrical Outlets

Electrical outlets make it easy to connect appliances and other energy receivers into a circuit and to disconnect them just as easily. ▼

◀ **Switches**

Switches let you open and close a circuit. If there were no switches in a circuit, the only way to control the flow of electricity would be to disconnect something. Imagine having to plug in a stove or TV set every time you wanted to turn it on.

Current Regulators

It is often necessary to regulate the amount of electric current in a circuit. For example, in a TV studio, it is necessary to be able to dim or brighten the lights. At home, you might want to raise or lower the volume of a radio or stereo receiver. The device used to regulate current in a circuit is called a rheostat (rē′ ə stat). ▶

How is electricity used?

Once electricity gets to the place where it is to be used, it is changed into another kind of energy, such as light, heat, sound, or motion. The devices that change electricity are energy receivers. A circuit can contain more than one energy receiver.

How many energy receivers can you think of? What does each one change the electricity into? Inventors are constantly finding new ways to use electric current. For example, there are electric pumps to milk cows and battery-powered robots that take out office trash at night.

The TV monitor above changes electricity into light energy. This energy is used to produce images on a TV screen.

A microphone is a device that changes sound into electrical energy. A speaker changes the electrical energy back into sound.

Light bulbs are devices that change electricity into light energy. What other kind of energy does a light bulb produce?

A TV camera uses electricity to run motors. The motors change electricity into energy of motion. Motors move the camera from place to place, focus the lens, and change the direction in which the camera is pointed.

How are you doing?

1. What are fuses and circuit breakers used for?
2. What are energy receivers?
3. **Think** Name three ways electricity is changed into another kind of energy in a TV studio. Name the devices that produce the change.

Where does electricity come from?

You have learned about electric current generated by cells and batteries. These sources of current are very important, but they are also quite limited. Imagine trying to operate all the electrical devices found in your home or in a TV studio using just batteries!

The electric energy used in homes, schools, factories, and TV stations is generated at an electric-power plant some distance from these places. It is carried from the power plant to the users by wire conductors called power lines.

The world's supplies of the fuels burned by power plants are running low. So everyone should help save energy. Turn off lights and appliances around the house when nobody is using them.

Power-Line Hazards

As electric current travels through overhead power lines, energy waves are given off.

Some people say that these low-energy waves may be harmful to people. Scientists and medical researchers are looking for possible links between these energy waves and some types of cancer. However, much more research needs to be done before any links can be proven.

Think About It Some people believe that power lines are dangerous to a person's health if they are too close to houses and schools. How could this problem be solved? Does your solution create other problems?

How is electricity transported?

Power plants make large amounts of electricity. Some power plants use the energy in moving water to make electricity. Some use nuclear energy. Most power plants burn fuels, such as coal or oil, to make electricity. Once electricity has been produced at a power plant, it must be transported to the people who use it.

The electricity that leaves the plant has a very high voltage. This means that the energy is very strong. High-voltage electricity is also dangerous.

Some factories can use high-voltage electricity just as it comes from the power plant. However, most users need electricity that has a lower voltage. So the high-voltage electricity is sent through a transformer. A transformer is a device that can change voltage. In this case, the transformer reduces the voltage.

Between the power plant and your home, electricity is sent through several transformers. Each time, the voltage is reduced. Transformers may be on power poles, in the ground, or in buildings that help distribute the electricity. The voltage of the electricity that reaches your home is high enough to run lights and appliances. But it is not so high that it burns out light bulbs or damages appliances.

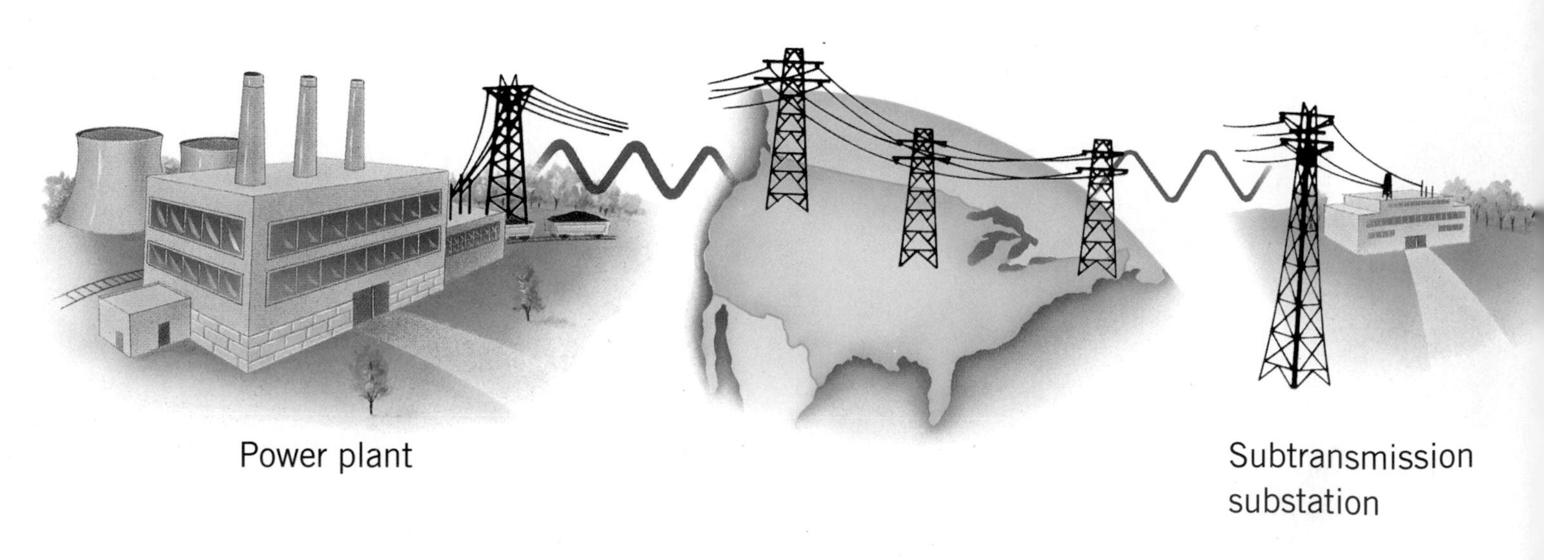

Career Corner

Electrician

I need to understand a lot about electricity. My name is Rodolfo Ortiz and I am a licensed electrician. Many technical schools offer courses in my field.

Part of my job is to set up electrical circuits in buildings or make repairs when something in an electrical system fails. Sometimes I install electrical devices. Because electric current can be dangerous, I need to know how electricity works and how it can be used before I can do my job.

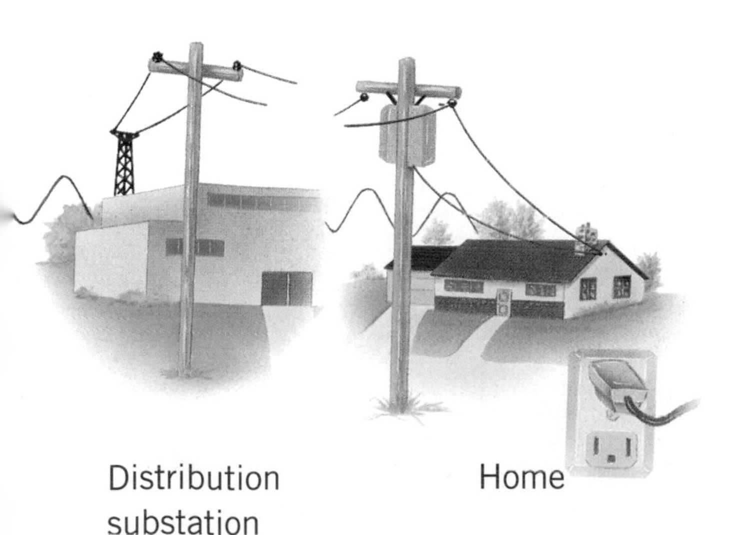

Distribution substation

Home

How are you doing?

1. How is electricity transported from the power plant to places where it is used?
2. How is the electricity that reaches your home different from the electricity that leaves a power plant? Why is it changed?
3. **Think** Give two reasons why batteries are not used to produce the electricity for use in the home.

Science & Literature Connection

EINSTEIN ANDERSON **SHOCKS** HIS FRIENDS

By Seymour Simon

This is a book about a boy who loves science. In this excerpt, Einstein deals with the class bully.

Einstein looked thoughtful. Would he have to fight Pat? His glasses slipped down over his nose, and he pushed them back with his finger. Suddenly he stood up. He pulled up the sleeves of his jacket. Then he rapidly began to pump his arms back and forth alongside his body as if he were running in a race.

"What are you doing?" asked Pat. "Are you going crazy?"

"Not a bit," said Einstein. "I just want you to see I have nothing up my sleeve. I'm about to give you the shock of your life."

Einstein brought up his arm and pointed his finger at Pat's nose. Suddenly a spark snapped from the tip of Einstein's finger to the tip of Pat's nose. Pat yelled and staggered back. In an instant he was in the back of the bus, trying to get as far away as possible from Einstein.

"That was great," (Einstein's brother) Dennis said. "You came to school all wired up?"

"No," said Einstein. "I just knew it was a good day for a spark."

Think About Your Reading

1. Use what you have learned about electricity. What caused that spark to zap Pat's nose?
2. Think about what you know about bullies. How do you predict Pat will treat Einstein from now on? Why?

Collecting data What kind of day is a "good day for a spark"? Rub your feet across a rug. Touch a doorknob. Record what happens. Also record weather conditions. Repeat each day for a week. What conclusions can you draw?

Where to Read More

Elaine Scott, *Ramona: Behind the Scenes of a Television Show* (William Morrow, 1988)

Lights! Camera! Action! Go backstage to see how a television show is made.

Looking Back

Words and Concepts

Match the description in Column A with the term in Column B.

Column A

1. A flow of charges through a conductor
2. Circuit in which all the parts are connected in a single path
3. Used to transport electricity from a power plant
4. A safety device in a circuit
5. Circuit with more than one path along which negative charges move
6. A device that separates positive and negative charges
7. A device that changes voltage

Column B

a. Series circuit
b. Power lines
c. Transformer
d. Fuse
e. Parallel circuit
f. Battery
g. Electric current

Applied Thinking Skills

Answer the following questions. You can use words, drawings, and diagrams in your answers.

8. How does a battery produce electricity?
9. What is one advantage of a parallel circuit over a series circuit?
10. **Your World** Suppose the electrical devices in your room stopped working all at once. What do you think could cause this? What would you do?

Show What You Know

How do you make a circuit tester?

Observe and Collect Data

1. Study your circuit board. Some of the foil you see through the holes is part of a complete circuit. Some is not.
2. Make a circuit tester by connecting the D-cell battery, wire, and bulb as shown. Test by inserting the ends of the two wires into separate holes.

Draw Conclusions

1. How can you tell when the foil under any two holes is part of the circuit?
2. Identify by number pairs of holes that are part of the same circuit.
3. Is this a parallel circuit or a series circuit? How can you tell?

Process Skills
Observing, Inferring

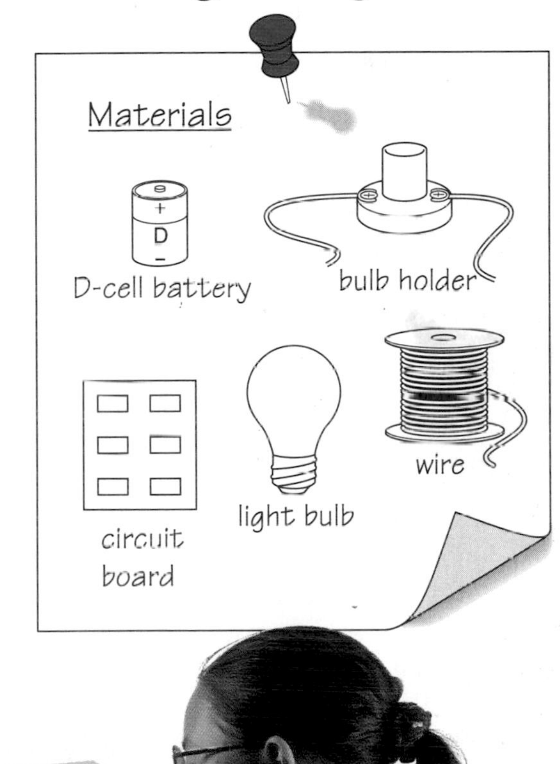

Chapter 3

Magnetism

Some television shows, especially sporting events, are broadcast live. The action you see on the screen is taking place as you watch it. However, most television shows today are taped.

The reels and cassettes in the picture hold videotape. Videotape is something like the film in a camera. It allows action shot by a television camera to be stored. The tape can then be played back later and viewed on a television screen. Videotape uses magnetism to store sounds and images. Magnetism is closely related to electricity.

Materials that have magnetism are attracted to certain other materials. Magnetism can be found in many places. For example, the earth shows magnetism. The core of the earth acts as if it contained a large magnet. Compasses react to the earth's magnetism.

Your body also has a tiny amount of magnetism. The electrical pulses that send messages to and from your brain create the magnetism.

In your Science Journal, list ways a kind of "tape" is used to store pictures, sound, or other information.

TOP
milk
rice
bread
rice
oranges
CAR

Explore Activity

What is attracted to magnets?

Hands-On Activity

Process Skills
Predicting, Communicating, Interpreting data

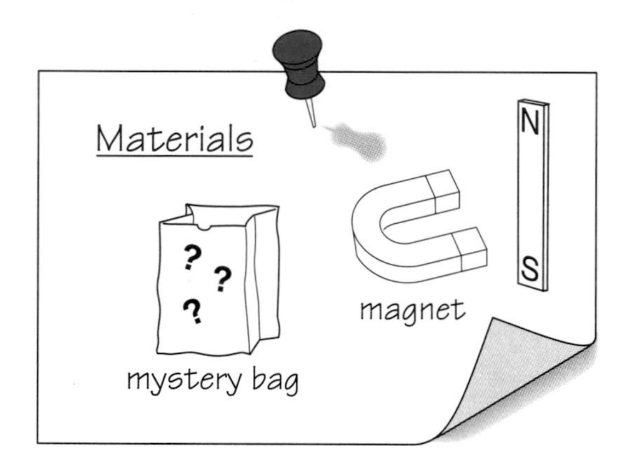

Observe and Collect Data

1. Remove the objects from your mystery bag.
2. ACTIVITY JOURNAL In your Activity Journal, make a chart with four columns. Label the columns from left to right in the following order: *Object, Material, Prediction,* and *Attracted (yes/no)*. List each object from your mystery bag in the left-hand column. In the second column, tell what material the object is made of.
3. **Predict** whether the object will be attracted to a magnet. Under the heading *Prediction*, write your prediction.
4. Use a magnet to check your predictions. Record the results in your chart under the column *Attracted (yes/no)*.

Share Your Results

Were your predictions accurate? Try to explain any predictions that were wrong. How did other groups' predictions compare with yours?

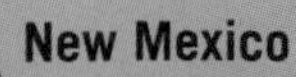

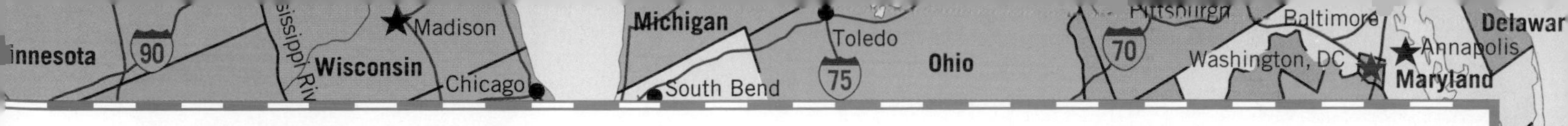

Draw Conclusions 

What kinds of materials are attracted to a magnet?

Apply What You Know

Are there any types of materials you did not test? If so, make a list of those materials. **Predict** which materials would be attracted to a magnet. If possible, get samples of those materials and check your predictions.

What is a magnet?

Have you ever heard someone described as having a "magnetic personality"? What do you think this means? Most people would say that it means that the person is popular or well liked. People are "attracted" to that person.

Any material that has magnetism is called a **magnet.** For this chapter, you will be using the magnets you are probably familiar with, such as the ones shown on this page.

A magnet's force of attraction is always strongest at its ends, or poles. A magnet has two poles, called north and south poles. Although you cannot see

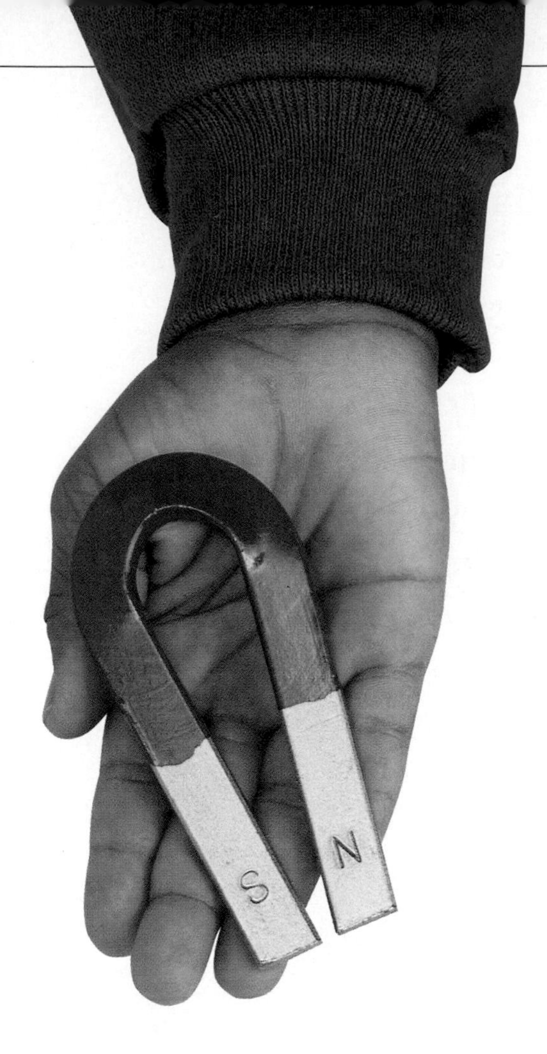

▲ Magnets can have any shape. A bar magnet and a horseshoe magnet are shown here. Other magnets are shaped like coins or balls. All magnets are surrounded by magnetic fields.

Find places at home or school where you use magnets. In your Science Journal, make a list and tell how the magnets are used. Share your information with your classmates.

BACK HOME

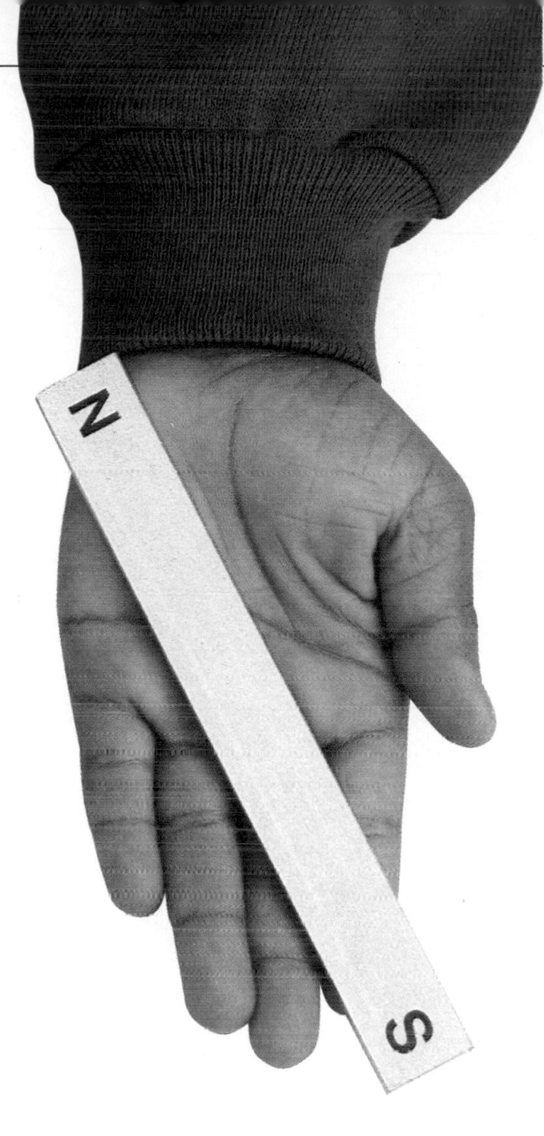

them, lines of force surround the poles. The area formed by these lines of force is called a **magnetic field**.

Magnetism is closely related to electricity. When two magnets are brought close to each other, the forces between them are similar to the forces between electric charges. Two like poles repel each other. Two unlike poles attract each other.

Be a Scientist

HANDS-ON ACTIVITY

What does a magnetic field look like?

1. Set two bar magnets on a flat surface so that their poles face the same direction. Place a sheet of wax paper over the magnets.
2. Carefully sprinkle some iron filings on the paper over the magnets. Jiggle the paper gently by tapping it. Observe the pattern formed by the iron filings.
3. ACTIVITY JOURNAL In your Activity Journal, draw the pattern formed by the iron filings.

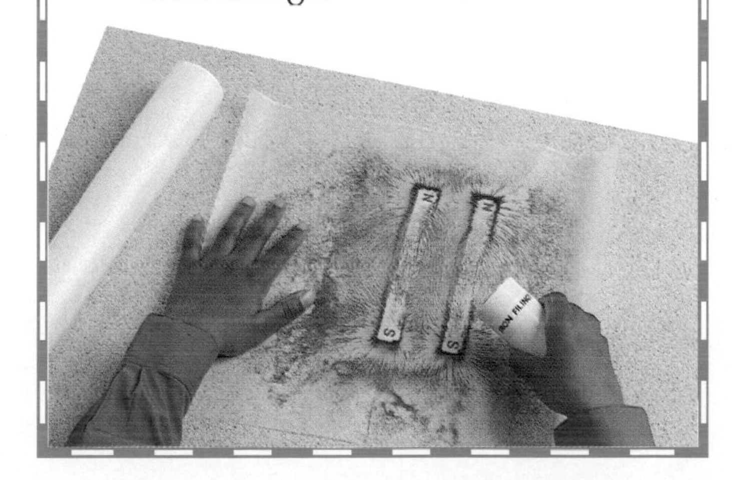

What is an electromagnet?

Some materials are natural magnets. Magnetite (mag´nə tīt), a type of iron ore, is a magnetic rock.

Some materials become magnetic when they are rubbed with a magnet. For example, if an iron nail is rubbed with a magnet, the nail becomes a weak magnet. However, its magnetism soon wears off.

Electricity also can be used to make a magnet. In the activity on the next page, you will make a device with an iron nail, wire, and battery. The iron nail becomes magnetic when the wire carries a current. This is called an **electromagnet**.

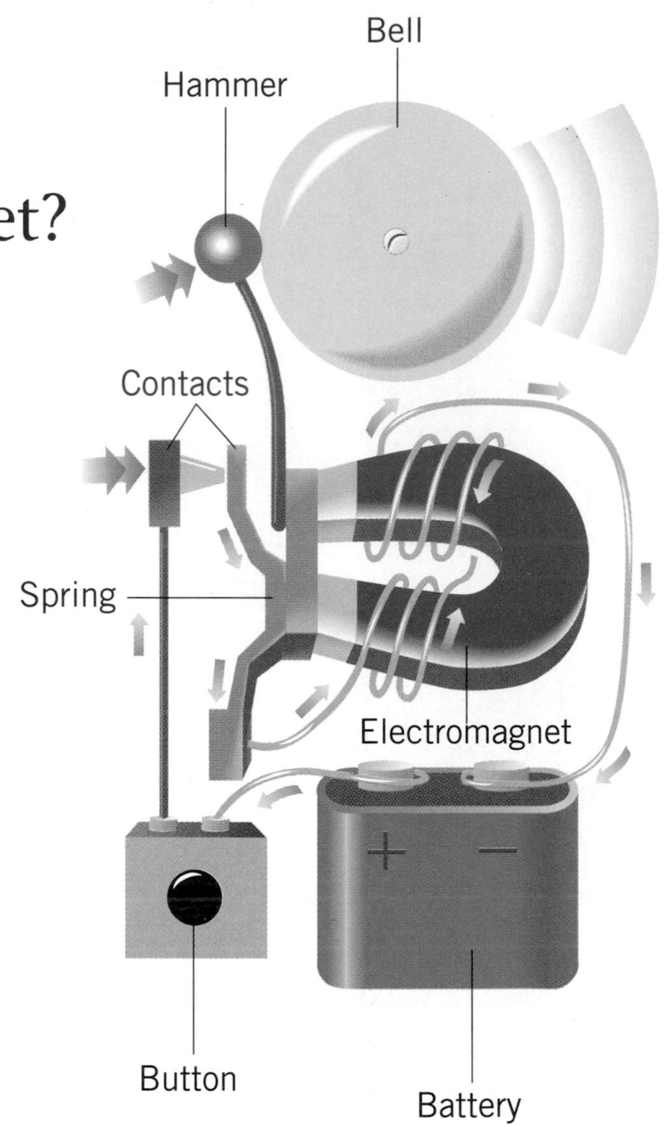

◀ A conductor carrying an electric current is surrounded by a magnetic field. This relationship between electricity and magnetism is used to make an electromagnet. Electromagnets are sometimes used in alarms and other electric bells.

Electromagnets are useful because their magnetism can be turned on and off by turning the current on and off. Some types of doorbells contain electromagnets. An example of an electromagnet in an electric bell is shown in the diagram.

By pressing the button, you complete the circuit and turn on the electromagnet. The base of the hammer (attached to a spring) becomes attracted to the electromagnet and quickly moves to it. The hammer strikes the bell. As soon as the base moves, the contacts stop touching and the circuit breaks. This turns off the electromagnet. The spring immediately pulls the hammer's base back, making the contacts touch again and turning on the electromagnet. The hammer moves and strikes the bell.

This process happens very quickly over and over again. The hammer repeatedly hits the bell, making it ring, as long as the button is pressed.

Be a Scientist

HANDS-ON ACTIVITY

How do you make electromagnets?

1. Wrap several coils of wire around an iron nail as shown.
2. Connect the ends of the wire to a D-cell battery. Try picking up some pieces of iron with the iron nail.

How are you doing?

1. What is a magnetic field? Where is it strongest?
2. People often say "opposites attract." Explain this saying in relation to magnets.
3. **Think** What are two things you might do to make an electromagnet more powerful?

Electric motors and videotapes in the TV studio editing room use magnetism.

How are magnets used?

One of the most important uses of electric current is in motors. An **electric motor** is a device that uses electricity to make objects move.

A motor contains a spinning electromagnet. This electromagnet lies between the poles of either a permanent magnet or a fixed electromagnet. The spinning electromagnet is attached to a shaft that can turn. Rapid changes in the direction of the current in the spinning electromagnet cause the shaft to turn. The turning shaft can be used to do work.

In a TV studio, motors are used to move equipment. Microphones on large booms move to follow the source of sounds. Cameras move and turn to keep track of the subjects being televised.

A motor uses an electromagnet to change electricity into motion.

TECHNOLOGY

Finding Metals Under Water

How would you find a sunken ship resting beneath hundreds of meters of ocean water? How would you find mineral deposits, such as iron ore, buried under layers of rock and soil?

Until a few years ago, it would have been a tough job. You would have had to dive down to search for the ship or dig test holes and blast rock to search for iron ore.

Today, scientists have a tool that makes their task much easier. The tool is a magnetometer (mag´nə täm´ət ər). This device detects variations in magnetic fields. Large areas of the earth's surface can be studied by scientists in a boat or in an airplane flying at a low altitude and towing a magnetometer.

Electromagnets also are used in some kinds of microphones and speakers. A microphone changes sound into electricity. The electric current that is produced flows through wires. When this current reaches a speaker, electricity is changed back into sound. In a TV studio, electromagnets are also used in videotape machines. These machines record pictures on videotape.

Videotape is made of a thin plastic film. The film is coated with iron oxide, a chemical that is easy to magnetize. TV cameras and microphones change light and sound into electric current, which is sent to the videotape machine. There current flows through electromagnets called heads. A motor moves the videotape past the recording head. This head magnetizes portions of the iron-oxide coating, producing a pattern on the videotape. Later, when the videotape is played back past the magnetic heads, electric current is produced. A television receiver changes this current into pictures and sound.

How are magnets used to make electricity?

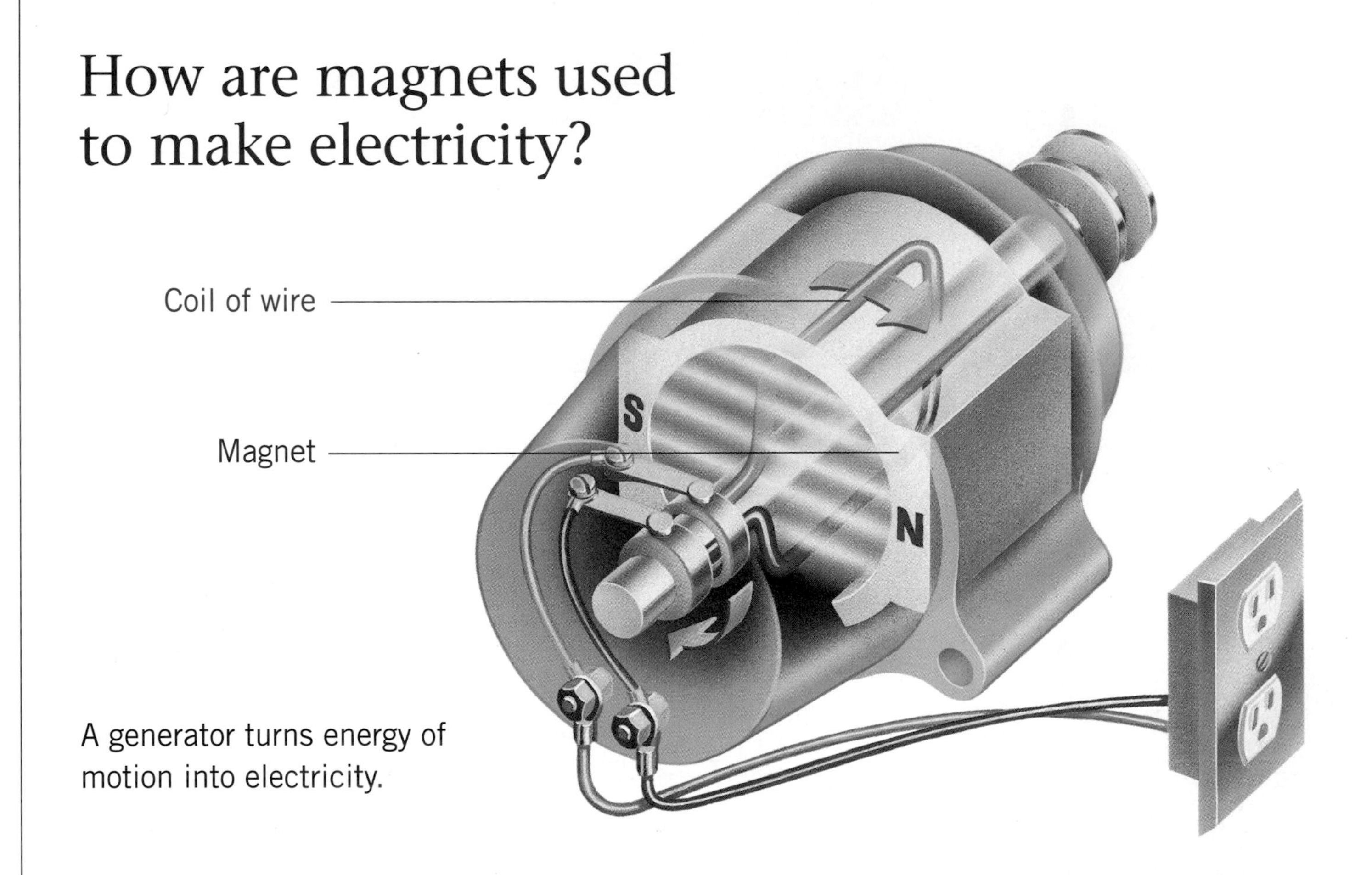

A generator turns energy of motion into electricity.

It is often useful to have a reliable source of electricity that can easily be moved from place to place. For example, dry cells and batteries provide electricity to operate flashlights and small portable appliances. Dry cells can be moved easily, but they produce little current and do not last long. Storage batteries produce more current, but they are large and heavy, and they need to be recharged often.

Think about what it would be like to lose power for several days. What would you and your family do? You would not have any lights or television. Your refrigerator would not keep food cold. You could not heat or cool the house. At such times, it would be useful to have a backup generator. A **generator** is a device that changes energy of motion into electricity.

A generator works by turning a coil of wire through a magnetic field. When the wire cuts across the magnetic lines of force, electric current is produced in the

Generators are needed when storms or other natural disasters knock down power lines.

wire. As long as the coil of wire turns, electric current is produced. Some source of energy, such as a gasoline engine, is needed to keep the coil of wire turning.

Natural disasters, such as hurricanes, fires, floods, and earthquakes, can cause power failure over a large area. Sometimes these failures, or blackouts, last for days or even weeks. During such times, generators can make the difference between life and death for people. Most hospitals, police stations, fire stations, and other emergency centers have back-up generators on hand. Many TV and radio stations also have generators to allow them to broadcast during an emergency.

How are you doing?

1. An electric motor changes electricity into what?
2. What keeps the coil of a portable generator turning?
3. **Think** What would happen if the permanent magnet in a generator lost its magnetism? Explain.

Looking Back

Words and Concepts

Complete the following statements.

1. Magnetism is closely related to _____.
2. Lines of force form a(n) _____ around a magnet.
3. A piece of iron can be _____ by rubbing it with a magnet.
4. _____ have magnetism that can be turned on and off.
5. An electric _____ uses electricity to make objects move by turning the current on and off.
6. A(n) _____ changes energy of motion to electricity.

Electromagnets are used to lift metal objects.

Applied Thinking Skills

Answer the following questions. You can use words, drawings, and diagrams in your answers.

7. Name three things needed to make an electromagnet.
8. Give two pieces of evidence that show that electricity and magnetism are closely related.
9. How are generators different from batteries? How are they similar?
10. **Your World** Small electric generators are available to power a bicycle light. How do you think these devices work?

Show What You Know

Which is stronger, push or pull?

Process Skills
Observing, Inferring

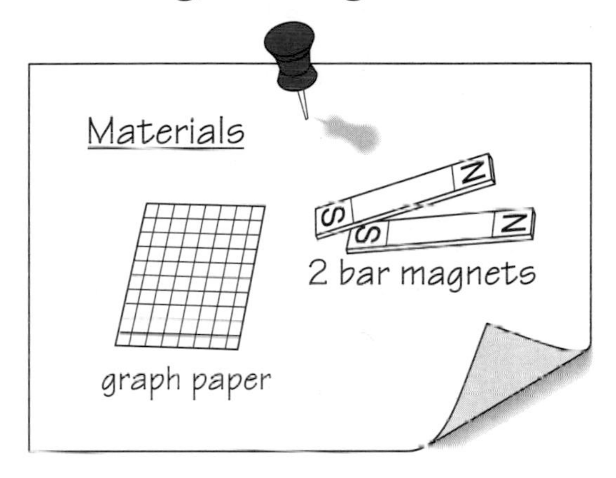

Observe and Collect Data

1. Place a sheet of graph paper on a flat surface. Set a bar magnet on the paper with the north pole of the magnet (marked *N*) facing toward you.
2. Place a second magnet on the graph paper with the south pole (marked *S*) facing toward the other magnet.
3. ACTIVITY JOURNAL Slowly slide the second magnet toward the first one. Observe the number of squares apart the magnets are when the first magnet starts to move. Record this number in your Activity Journal.
4. Turn one magnet around so that two like poles are facing each other. Repeat step 3.

Draw Conclusions

1. In step 3, did the magnets attract or repel each other? In step 4, did the magnets attract or repel each other?
2. Based on your observations, tell how like poles and unlike poles of two magnets affect each other.
3. Compare the force of attraction between the two magnets with the force of repulsion.

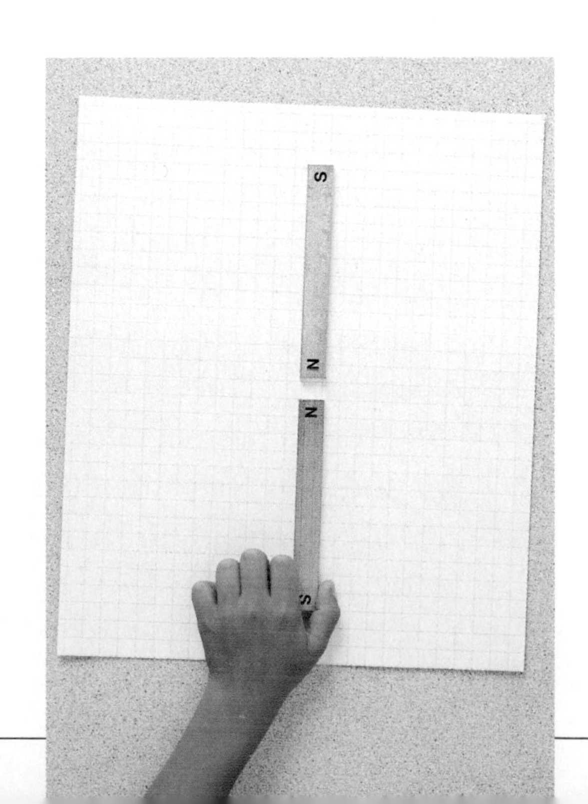

Electricity

Work by yourself, with a partner, or in a group. Select one activity to show what you know about electricity and magnetism.

Television Producer Organize a group of students to perform a comedy that explores the uses of magnetism and electricity.

News Writer Write a script for a television program or series that introduces its audience to electricity and magnetism.

Television Performer Create a funny character and use it to explain how electricity and magnetism are similar and how they are different. Videotape the performance to share with others.

Songwriter Write a rap song about electricity and magnetism. Include the sounds made by various electrical devices. Perform the song for the class.

Camera Operator Make a videotape or draw a mural showing different devices in your home that use electricity and magnetism. Identify each device and tell what it does and how it works.

Set Designer Make a model of a television studio. Label each of the devices found on the sound stage and in the control room and tell how each uses electricity and magnetism.

Glossary

circuit (ser´kit) A path along which negative charges move. (page C30)

conductor (kən duk´tər) Any material that allows negative charges to flow freely through it. (page C26)

electric cell (ē lek´trik sel) A device that separates positive and negative charges in a material. (page C28)

electric current (ē lek´trik ker´ənt) The flow, or movement, of negative charges through a conductor. (page C24)

electric motor (ē lek´trik mōt´ər) A device that uses electricity to make objects move. (page C54)

electromagnet (ē lek´trō mag´nit) A magnet produced by passing a current through a conductor wrapped around an iron core. (page C52)

generator (jen´ər āt´ər) A device that changes energy of motion to electricity. (page C56)

insulator (in´sə lāt´ər) Any material that does not allow negative charges to flow freely through it. (page C27)

magnet (mag´nit) Any material that has magnetism. (page C50)

magnetic field (mag net´ik fēld) The area formed by the lines of force that surround a magnet. (page C51)

parallel circuit (par´ə lel´ ser´kit) A circuit in which the parts are connected in separate branches. (page C32)

series circuit (sir´ēz ser´kit) A circuit in which the electricity follows a single path. (page C31)

static electricity (stat´ik ē´lek tris´i tē) An electric charge that collects, or builds up, on the surface of an object. (page C6)

Unit C Index

Boldface numerals denote glossary terms. Italic numerals denote illustrations.

Credits

Photographs

1 Tim Davis*; 2-3 Ken Karp*; 2BL Bob Daemmrich/Stock, Boston; 2TL George Hall/Woodfin Camp & Associates; 4 Ken Karp*; 5 Ken Karp*; 6-7 Ken Karp*; 7B Tom Ives/The Stock Market; 7T GHP Studio*; 8-12 Ken Karp*; 13 Tim Davis*; 15T Murray & Assoc./The Stock Market; 16R Anne Dowie*; 16T Ken Karp*; 17-19 Ken Karp*; 20-21 Ken Karp*; 21B Thomas Kitchin/Tom Stack & Associates; 23 Ken Karp*; 24B A. & J. Verkaik/The Stock Market; 24T Ken Karp*; 25-30 Ken Karp*; 31 Bruce Peterson/AllStock; 32-38 Ken Karp*; 41 Anne Dowie*; 44 Al Tielemans/Duomo; 45 Ken Karp*; 46-47 Ken Karp*; 47B Ken Karp*; 47R Ellis Herwig/Stock, Boston; 49-54 Ken Karp*; 57 Tom Myers/Photo Researchers; 58 G. Whiteley/Photo Researchers; 59 Ken Karp*

Special thanks to Bill Insley, Department of Physics and Astronomy, San Francisco State University and to KPIX-TV, San Francisco, California

*Photographed expressly for Addison-Wesley Publishing Company, Inc.

Illustrations

Jacque Auger 54, 56
Nea Bisek 8, 17, 19, 22, 45, 48, 59
Barbara Cousins 11, 52
Len Ebert 43
Carlyn Iverson 14–15, 38–39, 40–41
Shelton Leong 60–61
Jane McCreary 5, 9, 14, 23, 49

Text